IGNORANCE, A MODERN SLAVERY

"Therefore my people are gone into captivity because they have no knowledge."
Isaiah 5:13

Ignorance, A Modern Slavery
ISBN: 978-978-2954-78-7
Copyright© November 2019 by **Azubuike Bright**

For more information/ enquiries
Tel: +234 708 711 0990 0R +234 803 733 9684
Facebook: Azubuike Bright Ike
Instagram: officialbrightike

Published in Nigeria By: **Inspired to Aspire Media**
in collaboration with
The Light Technologies (TLT Print Media)
Tel: +234 703 346 0691, +234 808 199 7592
Email: thelighttechs4u@gmail.com

Contents

Dedication

I sincerely dedicate this book
to the Holy Spirit who
gives inspiration and
endowed me with
grace that makes
this book a
reality.

Acknowledgment

My sincere thanks goes to God Almighty, the Giver of inspiration who elected me by grace to establish His kingdom here on earth.

A wholehearted thanks to my mentor Pastor David Etaedafe for his efforts towards making my vision become a reality.

Special thanks to my Amazing family my Dad, Sir Azubuike Benjamin, Mummy Queen Azubuike and my siblings, Beauty Onyinyechi, Wisdom , Destiny and Favour, for there love and encouragement, I owe you more than you expect.

I cannot forget Mr. Mike Adeyinka, the director of The Light Technologies (TLT Print Media) and his team of Editors; you are all amazing; I'm grateful!

I must say a big thank you to my circle of friends at school /home, especially, Amadi Daniel Kelechi, Ogbwoo Emmanuel and Ogbodah Gift who were around during final editing you all are amazing.

Finally, I want to say thank you Lord Jesus for everything you have done during this process and beyond. I will forever serve you.

Introduction

The major problem of the globe today is tied down to ignorance, which is a major hindrance and setback to human success in the world.

The problem of Christianity today is not the devil or poverty; it is ignorance and the power of your mind. Ignorance is the powerful chain that has held many Christians under mighty bondage that has made them despise knowledge and embrace massive failure which is ignorance.

The universe today has been covered by the canopy of ignorance which has made life difficult and frustrating, making humans living a life of slavery without physical chains but chains of the mind. This is the greatest slavery of the globe today and it will shock you that "Ignorance is the greatest killer of man's potential."

Our ability to accept knowledge makes us unique in

life and free from the chains of our mind, thereby causing us to do exploits and embrace success in this world. This is what God has destined us here on earth.

The major causes of poverty and setback today are borne out of ignorance of the right word. This has hindered many humans in the globe from actualizing their great potentials here on earth.

God Almighty, our Creator and Father has endowed Christians and children of God with abundance resources to make them exceedingly great here on earth to do exploit and succeed in all areas of their lives, but ignorance has covered their eyes thereby subjecting them to the chains of poverty and stress in life.

But I decree over your life!
As a son of God, as you read this book *Ignorance a modern Slavery*, you shall come out of stress and frustration and the chains of ignorance in your life shall be broken, in Jesus' Name. Amen.

Chapter 1

IGNORANCE IS SLAVERY

*I*gnorance is a modern slavery that has kept men and women of great potentials captive and under supernatural chains in this modern time causing you not to do exploits and go forward in life.

Ninety-five percent of the problems of the world today is ignorance. For example, our country, Nigeria, is blessed, and so blessed that we lack no natural resources, but ignorance has eaten deep into the fabrics of our leaders who don't see any usefulness in petroleum apart from exporting it to knowledgeable countries, for them to use that same petroleum to produce other products and export it back to Nigeria for huge amounts of dollars.

Come to think of it, petroleum can be used to produce other things, but our leaders choose darkness which is ignorance, instead of light which is knowledge.

- A wise man once said, **"Behind every struggle in life it is the function of ignorance."**
- A pastor, Sam Adeyemi once said, **"Place value on information so you can be free from oppression."**

Ignorance is the father of oppression, which has oppressed Christians for their lack of knowledge. Our greatest challenge in life is not the devil but ignorance, and the devil plays in line with our ignorance gradually and eventually holds us captive under supernatural chains of the mind.

Hear this and hear it well! Jesus resisted temptation from the devil because He has the knowledge of God's Word.

The devil is a PIG
P   -   Play
I   -   Inline
G   -   Gradually

The devil plays in line gradually with our ignorance, thereby causing us to suffer and experience struggles in life. Let us prepare a funeral for ignorance; let us go for knowledge.

Here this good news: The moment you have the

knowledge of God's Word the devil loses contact with you.

About ninety percent of Christians who are poor today are covered with the canopy of intellectual darkness which is ignorance. The Scripture in Hosea 4:6 says,

" My people are destroyed for lack of knowledge because thou has rejected knowledge."

"The Word of God is the greatest book of knowledge."

There is nothing in this world that is not in the Holy Bible. As a genuine child of God, you are expected to be successful, because as a born again you are not expected to be poor, but ignorance has covered the mind of Christians with darkness.

To be free from ignorance, you must turn to knowledge to be free from the chains of poverty. You become a slave by accepting the chains of ignorance and neglecting the power of freedom which is Right Knowledge.

"All knowledge, is knowledgeable but right

knowledge is preferable."
Ignorance has the power of captivity; not physical captivity but emotional captivity which leads to poverty, setback, frustration and failure in life. Hear this! Ignorance is dangerous and a great pollution of the world, and every child of God needs to embrace knowledge so as not to be affected by the disease of ignorance.

The Scripture in 1 Peter 2:2A says
"For if they have escaped the pollution of the world through knowledge of the Lord."

God's Word is the ultimate of all knowledge. Also, in Isaiah 5:13A the Scripture says,
"Therefore my people are gone into captivity because they have no knowledge."

If you are ignorant of God's Word you are under powerful chains that only the knowledge of God's Word can destroy.

A writer, Thomas Pynchon, once said, **"Ignorance is not just a blank space on a person, mental man; it has contours and coherence, and for all I know rules of operation as well."**

- Ignorance of God's Word is a powerful tool that hinders man's breakthrough in life.
The Scripture says "The knowledge maketh one wise and to be wise makes you to inherit God's glory but ignorance shall be the promotion of fools."

You become fools by accepting darkness (ignorance) and neglecting light which is the knowledge of God's Word.

Ignorance is the modern slavery, that has endangered and corrupted the mind of children of God and our ability to go for knowledge, open the foundation of our potential, and cause us to do exploits.

"The moment you reject ignorance, you open the door for knowledge which will yield massive success and expansion in life."

Ignorance Destroys Man's Dignity
Ignorance is very harmful to man, and is capable of destroying man's dignity and rendering him useless. It is very easy to be ignorant and not knowing that you are ignorant. Many of us often make the mistake of acting on an assumption that proves to be wrong, but makes little sense at that moment, but that little sense eventually becomes totally wrong.

This kind of ignorance destroys mans dignity and renders him stagnant in life. Without the knowledge of the right word life makes no sense. To improve your life you must improve your mind with the knowledge of the right word to enable you lay a solid foundation for the future. Hear this! Remaining in a state of ignorance can lead to serious economic downfall, relationship crises, thereby destroying and rendering the dignity of a man useless, because he does not know the next step to take to be successful, and does not want to know, thereby wallowing in abject confusion, stagnation and frustration in life.

Right knowledge is required to be free from the chains of ignorance.

Chapter 2
THE NATURE of IGNORANCE

*I*gnorance is the perfect killer of man's potentials, goals and career here on earth.

Wikipedia defines ignorance as lack of knowledge. It also describes ignorance as a state of person being unaware and can describe individuals who are deliberately ignorant and disregard important information or fact.

An ignorant person is clamorous, simple and knows nothing, has no intention to know and can never attain a great height in life, except he/she embraces knowledge.

Hear this! An ignorant person suffers poverty because he deals with a slack hand but a knowledgeable person makes rich.

There are certain consequences of living an ignorant life. They are stipulated below.

I. Ignorance kills a man's potential

Ignorance is the perfect killer of a man's potential that holds the man captive and kills his potential. An ignorant person is under powerful chains only knowledge can break the chains.

Everyone has a unique potential which makes him/her different from other persons, but the ability to discover one's potential through the right knowledge makes one different from others. Ignorance plays a vital role in killing man's potential.

The spirit of ignorance will blind your mind making you fill like you have no potential in you. But the power of knowledge will help you realize that you have outstanding qualities that will make you great in life.

Hear this! Without the right knowledge, your potential can never be discovered and developed. And when your potential is not discovered, such potential is dead and is not better than the fig tree in the Bible that did not discover its purpose on earth.

Life Story

Long ago, I was so ignorant that I believed that man

does not have any unique potential in him to make him attain a great height. I felt like our degrees in the university cam make one great in life. I was so confused with life.

Towards July 2018, I realized that the right Knowledge makes rich, I discovered that true knowledge of God's word and the knowledge of relevant materials will help in discovering and unveiling the great and hidden potential in my life.

I started working towards developing myself. I borrowed a book from my mentor. That book, coupled with the knowledge of God's Word, which is the Holy Bible, brought me out of inferiority complex, broke the chains of ignorance in my life, and unveiled my potentials.

I hungered for knowledge. I read little books including a book by Rich Warren *Purpose Driven Life*.
That book turned my story around and helped me discover my God given potential to be a great author.

To be successful, and break the yoke of ignorance in life, right knowledge is required for one to discover and fulfil one's God-given purpose.

ii. Ignorance makes one blind inside

Ignorance is a mighty cloth, that has covered the mind of great   men and women, making them captive under supernatural chains of poverty and stagnation, ignorance also makes them ignore the truth which is light and   rather embrace darkness which is ignorance.

Ignorance plays a vital role to close the minds of humans towards attaining greater height in life. Ignorance is the father of stagnation in life.

True Life Story By A Wise Man

A fisher man, went for fishing every morning at exactly 7 o'clock to catch fish to feed his family and sell some to generate income for himself. He made money every day.

Whenever he caught small ones he felt happy, put them in his bag and took them home. He fried some of the fish and sold the rest. But whenever he caught big fish he got angry and threw them back into the river.

One morning, a man saw him throwing the big fish back into the water and keeping the small one in his bags. The man was amazed and asked the fisherman why was he throwing the big fish back into the water.

The fisherman replied, Sir only the small fish can enter my frying pan at home. The big fish cannot enter the frying pan, let alone frying.

The elderly man laughed and told him that he could cut the big fish into pieces and fry them, have enough to eat and sell the rest. After hearing this, the fisherman hugged the old man and cried out having realized he had been under chains of ignorance.

Hear this and hear it well! Ignorance is a perfect modern slavery that has kept men of great potentials under chains and making them blind at the inside.

The fisherman was ignorant, but the moment the chains of ignorance was broken through the right knowledge given to him by the elderly man he realized the truth and experienced a relief. He became ready to move to a greater height.

You must believe you are blessed and born to win, without struggling because God has given us all we need to be outstanding in life. Just go for the right knowledge to actualize success in life.

iii.   **Ignorance Makes one Inferior**
Ignorance of God's Word makes you feel inferior to

your friends, relatives, neighbours and those of greater status.

The moment you go for knowledge, the chains of ignorance will be broken. You will discover that there is no difference between black and white men, Jew or Greek, male or female, and that everyone is equal in the sight of God despite our status or position.

The Scripture in Romans 10:12 says

"For there is no difference between the Jew and the Greek, for the same Lord over all is rich unto all that call upon Him."

As a child of God, the moment you realize and understand this scripture and meditate on it, you must live an outstanding life of success and wealth.

Inferiority complex is a deadly disease that has made many Christians not to move forward in life, because they have been covered with the canopy of ignorance, But with knowledge of the right word we can conquer ignorance. and I pray as you go for the right word, that success will locate you, in Jesus' Name.

Hear this in Job 13:2
*"What ye know, the same do I know also,
I am not inferior unto you."*

Iv. Ignorance Destroys Man's Dignity

Ignorance is very harmful to man, and is capable of destroying man's dignity and rendering him useless. It is very easy to be ignorant and not knowing that you are ignorant. Many of us, as being mentioned earlier, often make the mistake of acting on an assumption that proves to be   wrong, but makes little sense   at that moment, but that little sense eventually becomes totally wrong.

This kind of ignorance destroys man's dignity and renders him stagnant in life.

Without knowledge of the right word life makes no sense. To improve   your life, you must improve your mind with the knowledge of the right word, to enable you lay a solid foundation for the future. As has been mentioned earlier, remaining in a state of ignorance can lead to serious e c o n o m i c d o w n f a l l a n d relationship crises thereby destroying and rendering the dignity of a man useless, because he does not know the next step to take to be successful and does not want to know. This   leads him into wallowing in abject confusion, stagnation and frustration in life.

Right knowledge is required to be free from the chains of ignorance.

There are certain foundational causes that hinders people from actualizing their great potentials. Some of these causes include:

1. **Traditional Beliefs and False Proverbs**
Traditional beliefs and false proverbs are great giants that have held great men and women captive under supernatural chains, thereby subjecting them to the chains of poverty and making them stagnated in life.

Traditional beliefs and false proverbs are the foundations of poverty and the major causes of ignorance in the globe. False proverbs have thrown many individuals into abject confusion and have made them wallow in total confusion.

Some of the false proverbs include

"Heaven helps those who help themselves."

Hear this! This proverb is typically wrong. Heaven only helps those who cannot help themselves, because if you can help yourself, there is no reason for heaven to help you. Some people say this to get spiritual help or go to ocultic places. They use this proverb to justify themselves because they are ignorant of the right Word of God.

Another false proverb is "Money is the root of all evil." The scripture does not say money is the root of all evil but it say in
1 Timothy 6:10a, the Scripture says,
**"For the love of money is
the root of all evil."**

The Scripture clearly says the love of money is the root of all evil; not that money is the root of all evil. Our people today have let themselves led astray by this falseful proverb that makes them fill that making money is a sin. Instead of going for the right knowledge and making money, they rely on a false proverb to justify their poverty by saying money is the root of all evil.

Hear this! Poverty is a great offence in the sight of God, because God has blessed the earth and the people in it with exceedingly great potentials and talents to enable them become wealthy and do exploits.

"The level of knowledge you get determines the level of wealth you get."

The Scripture says,
> *"Occupy till I come." It does not say suffer*
> *till I come. Occupy means take control,*
> *take charge and be wealthy.*

Hear this! Only the right knowledge can guarantee you success.

ii. Lack of Understanding

Lack of understanding is one of the principal causes of ignorance that has played vital role to hinder men and women of great potentials from doing exploits.

Pastor David Ibiyeomie once said *"If you don't have understanding you can't be outstanding."*
The moment you don't have an understanding of the right words that will cause positive changes in your life, failure and stagnation will start knocking at your door.

To be great in life, deep understanding of the right word is required.

Life Story
Towards May 2018, I listened to a man of God preaching about tithing and I got a deep understanding of the message on tithing.
With all humility, since that day, I started practising it till now, I have not been under financial stress, just because I got a deep understanding about Tithing.

It is important to note that you can only do well in what you understand.

Ignorance is a strong bond that causes people not to have understanding, thus making them not to be outstanding in life.

Hear this truth!
If you don't have an understanding of being a success, you will always fail in life. Likewise, if you don't have a deep understanding of being wealthy watch out for the next step of poverty in your life.

Your understanding of the right word can destroy the strong chains of ignorance in your life and I decree over your life as you go for the right word and have an understanding of it, that chains of ignorance shall be broken, in Jesus' Name.

iii.   **Lack of Studying**

Lack of studying is typically being in the state of ignorance, because you don't want to go for new knowledge on how to develop yourself. To build yourself in life, study is required.

"Without study you can't be steady in life."

The scripture in 2Timothy 2:15, says

>**"*Study to show thyself approved.*"**

Without constant study you can't come out from the powerful chains of ignorance. To be successful in life, constant study is required to enable you attain great heights in life.

iv. **Blind Nature of The Mind**

>**"The mind is the goal-post of your life".**

Ignorance makes one blind at the inside and the moment you are blind inside, all your thoughts in life are channelled towards the negative direction.

To be great in life and be free from the powerful chains of ignorance you need to set your mind towards the positive direction.

The Scripture in Roman 12:2A says,

>**"*And be not conformed to this world, but be ye transformed by the renewing of your mind.*"**

Your capacity to renew your mind helps you to renew your destiny, and once your destiny is renewed the devil loses contact with you, and the yoke of ignorance is broken.

Hear this in Proverb 23:7!
"For as a man thinketh in his mind, so he is."

Everything in your hand today is as a result of the function of your mind, because your mind defines your goal.
A great man once said, *"Your imagination sets a base for your destination."*
Renewing your mind is the perfect way to be free from the bondage of ignorance.

CONSEQUENCES OF LIVING AN IGNORANT LIFE

There are certain great and powerful consequences of living an ignorant life. Some of these consequences are listed and explained below.
i. **Poverty**
Poverty is the foundational cause of ignorance.
Living an ignorant life has made many poor individuals in the globe believe that they are destined by God to be poor or that being a poor is living a righteous life. These beliefs have made them

feel that God wants them to be   poor; that if God wants them to be rich He will make   them.

Hear this! Nobody is born poor, but the level and degree of knowledge we gather towards developing ourselves determines the outcome of life for us, whether to be poor or wealthy.

God cannot make you rich when your mind is still covered by poverty. Until you go for the right knowledge that will enlighten your mind about poverty, you can never be wealthy.

God is a wealthy God and as such we being his children are also wealthy, because we were created in the same image and likeness of God. We have all it takes to be great on earth, but we need to go for t h e right knowledge to enable us do exploits and commit ourselves to hard work, and riches will be ours.

God is faithful to all who call upon Him and He is God over the poor and   the rich, the Greek and the Jew.

The Scripture in Romans 10:12B says, "For the same Lord over all is rich unto all that call upon him."

God wants you to be rich and enjoy life to the fullest, but living an ignorant life can make you not to enjoy

life here on earth. Also in 1Timothy 6:17 the Scripture says,
> *"Charge them that are rich in this word, that*
> *They may be not high minded, nor trust in*
> *uncertain riches, <u>but in the living</u>*
> *<u>God who giveth us richly</u>*
> *<u>all things to enjoy</u>."*

Only the right knowledge of God's Word can guarantee you success in your life. To break the chains of poverty the right knowledge of God's Word is required.

ii. **Stagnation**

Being stagnated in life is as a result of living an ignorant life, because the moment you are living an ignorant life, there is no room for you to learn and discover new ideas for you to move forward and attain a great height in life.

Being stagnant means being static, not developing or growing. Therefore, being stagnant in life is ceasing to develop in life, advance in careers or to become idle. This is the function of living an ignorant life.

Individuals and nations are stagnated today not because they are not blessed with resources which will help them move to a greater height, but because they are ignorant of the right knowledge that will help them attain that height and position in life which they wish to attain.

Success is not all about spoken words; success is action. Without the right knowledge about success, you can never be librated from the chains of poverty.

iii.   Frustration

Frustration in life is caused by ignorance of the right words, because the moment you have the right knowledge that will change and turn your situations around, you can never be frustrated in life; rather you will be happy in life.

To be frustrated means to be stopped or disappointed, suffering from frustration, dissatisfied, agitated and discontent because one is unable to perform an action or fulfil a desire.

The moment you are frustrated in life, life makes no meaning to you, this happens because you are super-naturally chained by ignorance which had made you a slave in modern time.

Only the right knowledge can enable you not to be

frustrated with life and be happy and attain your desired point, in life.

And I decree that as you go for the right knowledge, frustration will be eliminated from your life in Jesus' Name.

iv. Feeling Inferior in Life

To feel inferior in life is a function of living an ignorant life, because when you go for the right knowledge you will discover that there is no difference between a white man and a black man. The only difference is the way they position their minds.

Your mind is a channel to your destiny, the moment you position your mind in life, you can go to any part of the world and you will be recognized as a great man or woman in the society. But only the right knowledge of God that can help you develop your mind towards breaking the chains of ignorance that has made you captive under the power of inferiority.

The Holy Bible is the greatest book of wisdom and greatest book of inspiration given to you by God to help you break the powerful chains of ignorance which has become a modern form of slavery.

The Scripture in Romans 10:12 says,

"For there is no difference between the
Jew and the Greek; for the same
Lordover all is rich unto all
That call upon Him."
When you go for the knowledge of the right word
and discover this Scripture, the chains of inferiority
complex will give way for success to come in.

Hear this! Despite the fact that you are born poor or
you are black, purple or brown in colour, you are all
equal in the sight of God and the moment you call
upon Him, He will grant you your heart desires,
irrespective of your ranks, because God is the same
Lord over all that call upon Him.

And as you call upon the Lord genuinely, the powers
of inferiority complex in your life shall be broken, in
Jesus' Name.

Chapter 4

PRINCIPLES TO CONQUERING IGNORANCE

There are certain guidelines in life and when such principles are neglected, it results in death.

There is a general principle of crossing the road. Before you cross, you look left and right, then you can cross and this principle is the best, but when the principle is neglected it results in accident.

Hear this: There are certain powerful principles of conquering ignorance in life, but when this principles are neglected, the chain of ignorance can never get off our neck in life. These principles are clearly explained below.

i.   **Locate God's Word**

Locating God's Word is the basic principle towards conquering ignorance. The Holy Bible is the greatest book of knowledge which God has given to us free of charge and there is nothing which has happened or is happening on earth that is not in the Bible. This is to prove to you that the Word of God is worth more than riches.

Hear this! There are many secrets in the Bible which include:
a.   The secret of success is in the Word of God;
b.   Secret of prosperity;
c.   Secret of Riches and Wealth;
d.   Secrets of breaking the yoke of poverty;
e.   Secrets of breaking the chains of ignorance, and much more.

The Word of God is so powerful that the moment you discover the right word, you recover from your challenges in life.
The Scripture in Isaiah 5:13 says,
> *"Therefore my people are gone into captivity because they have no knowledge."*

The Word of God here clearly explains that you are under the chains of ignorance because you neglected the Word. Only the word of God can restore your freedom and make you successful once again.
When you locate the Word you find God, and when you find God the chains of ignorance in your life will be broken. The moment you ignore the Word of God,

there will be a vacuum of success in your life, which will eventually be replaced by failure.
The scripture in 1 Timothy 4:15 says,

*"Meditate upon these things; give
thyself wholly to them; that thy
profiting may appear to all."*

The moment you understand God's Word, you discover that it will be profitable to you, and the powerful chains of ignorance will be broken in your life. Also in 2 Peter 1:3,

*"According as His divine power hath given
unto us all things that pertain unto life
and godliness, through the <u>knowledge
of Him</u> that called us to
glory and virtue."*

Hear this: Christianity was not designed for struggling but for prosperity. The power of ignorance, however, has made many individuals believe that they are destined to suffer. This is wrong. Only God's Word can break that yoke, and I decree as you go for God's Word that negative yoke and chain shall be destroyed, in Jesus' Name.

In Numbers 23:19 Scripture says,

"God is not a man that He should lie, neither
the Son of Man, that He should repent;
hath He said, and shall He not do it?
or hath He spoken and shall He
Not make it good?"

God can never lie, and His Word shall never return void, there is nothing in the Bible that will not come to pass because God is not a man.

Hear this and hear it well! To break the mighty chain of living an ignorant life, God's Word is needed to be put in place in your mind, heart and your soul, to guarantee your freedom from living an ignorant life. Your ability to search for God's Word helps you to gather wealth to enable you become successful and free from the chains of ignorance in your life.

ii.   **Go for Knowledge**

Knowledge is the most powerful tool on earth that can destroy the chains of ignorance and make one free from the bondage of slavery. Knowledge is the perfect solution on to breaking the chains of ignorance and other dozens related problem which may has arise as a result of living an ignorant life. Knowledge lights up the dark corners of ignorance by restoring perfection in one's light.

Knowledge can simply be said to be having awareness of a particular fact or situation, or being informed or made aware of something. It can also be a collection of existing information that may be found in written or oral form.

It may consist of data information and other relevant information needed by the researcher. True knowledge has the capacity capacity of breaking the yoke of ignorance in your life.

Hear this! The most important knowledge on the face of the earth is the knowledge of God and His laws, because with the knowledge of God's Word success and prosperity is guaranteed, and the keys of breaking the yoke of ignorance is in God's law. In order to have knowledge about God and His law you need to study the Bible.

The Word of God helps you to change from ignorance to wisdom. The greatest gift of God is the Word of God. When you study the Bible you operate in a supernatural level which is from

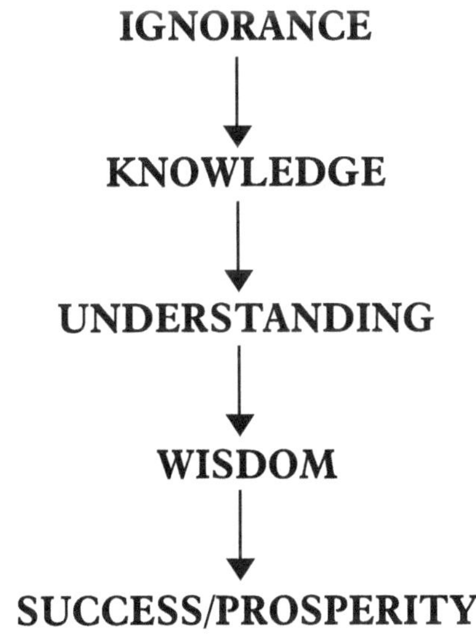

You need to realise that there is difference between knowledge, understanding and wisdom. Knowledge is what you know through studying but understanding is a deeper level of seeing how knowledge can work, while wisdom is the ability to make sound judgement to take that knowledge and understanding and apply them.

We must now stay knowledgeable in the ways of God through prayer. Knowledge is the principal thing for which the principal of prosperity is broken, without knowledge you cannot attain greater height on earth.

Here this: **"All knowledge is knowledgeable but right knowledge is preferable."** Basically there are two types of knowledge which are:

a.   **Right Knowledge (Relevant Knowledge)**
This is the required knowledge which one needs to apply to enable him or her to be liberated from his or her negative situation.

Hear this! Every frustration and confusion in life is as a result of ignored principle. If you want to be successful in life and break the mighty chains of ignorance, you need to go for the right knowledge, study books about prosperity and the word of God and other relevant books and the chains of ignorant will be broken.

"All knowledge is always knowledgeable but the right one is preferable."

If you want to be successful in business, you need to read books on great business men like Bill Gate, Aliko Dangote and many others. You can't read *Things Fall Apart* and expect the yoke of ignorance to be broken in your business and career.

Hear this! Only Right knowledge can liberate you

from poverty and break the yoke of ignorance in your life, and I decree as you apply the right knowledge towards your academics and career, that you shall be liberated from stress to wealth, from nothing to plenty, in Jesus' Name.

ii.   Wrong Knowledge

This kind of knowledge often leads to destruction and abject frustration. This is often known as irrelevant knowledge and can only come to you when you are made captive by the chains of ignorance, which has made you subject to negativity. A situation whereby some people are wallowing in poverty instead of study about prosperity and success; and studying the Holy Bible which will give them the needed knowledge, they choose to go for the wrong knowledge of armed robbery, cultism, kidnapping, because their eyes have been covered with the canopy of ignorance. This will eventually lead to untimely death, because it is the wrong knowledge which was applied and which will result in untimely death.

Hear this good news! Only right and relevant knowledge can liberate you from abject confusion and frustration and lead you to promotion and success. I decree as you apply the right knowledge in your career, academics, ministry and in all your life endeavours that you shall be successful in life, in Jesus' Name. Amen.

HOW TO OBTAIN TRUE KNOWLEDGE

Knowledge is the principal thing in life and there are possible ways of getting lasting knowledge which is capable of bringing you out of darkness and relieving you from the stress of ignorance, and breaking the chains of ignorance. Some of the keys for obtaining true knowledge will be discussed below.

1.   **Through God's Word:** Only God and His Word gives true and lasting knowledge here on earth, without God you have no base in life. The Scripture in 1 Corin 12:18 say,

> *"For to one, is given the Holy Spirit*
> *the word of wisdom, to another*
> *the word of knowledge*
> *by the same Spirit."*

Only the Spirit of God can guarantee knowledge and wisdom and will help in all areas of life and career to produce lasting exploits in life.
Also 2 Chronicle 1:2A says,

*"Wisdom and knowledge is
granted unto thee."*

Also in Proverb 2:6 the scripture says,

***"For the Lord gives wisdom, out of his
mouth cometh knowledge
and understanding."***

Only God's Word guarantees perfect knowledge and understanding which can help in breaking the chains of ignorance.

The scripture in Jeremiah 11:18 tells us,

***"And the Lord hath giveth me knowledge
of it; and I know it, then thou
Shewdst me their doings."***

Only the Word of God guarantees knowledge in all areas of life, and without God's Word in your heart you can't go far in life.

b.   **Learning:** Your ability to learn guarantees how much you can earn in life. Knowledge is gain through learning, and the process of adding new information to an existing store guarantees more knowledge. We learn to discover and recover our life. You learn to discover certain chains of ignorance holding you captive and the possible ways of destroying ignorance in your life.

C.   **Studying:** Studying is a continuous process in life. To go far in life, study is always required to enable you to break the chains of ignorance.

The Scripture in 2 Timothy 2:15A tells us,

"Study to shew thyself approved..."

To achieve great success, constant study of God's Word is required. Also study of relevant materials is required in the area were you are ignorant of.

We study to develop our minds towards the right direction of life. Studying can seriously damage ignorance, thereby relieving us of the chains of poverty, stress, frustration and struggles of life.

Lyndon Baines Johnson once said, **"A book is the most effective weapon against intolerance and ignorance."**

Hear this! Studying helps you to be enlightened in life, and without books you can't be backed up in life. Studying is one of the vital endeavours that enable you to live a free life without chains. And as you study, the chains of ignorance will be broken beyond recognition, in Jesus' Name.

d.   Conducting Research

Conducting research is a perfect pillar that clears away doubt in your heart and brings you out of the bondage of ignorance. This is one of the vital activities to embrace to enable you conquer ignorance in your life.

e.   Asking Questions and Asking the Right Individuals

A proverb once says, *"He that asked questions never goes astray."*

Asking questions and asking the right individuals help you to be directed in life and not be under the chains of ignorance which is the result of not asking questions.

Once you ask questions, you discover the truth; and the moment you discover the truth, the chains of ignorance will be broken in your life.

F.   Kill Pride and Stay Humble

Pride is a pillar of ignorance that has many great men and women become captives under mighty supernatural chains.
The Scripture in Proverbs 11:2 says,

> *"When pride cometh, then cometh shame,*
> *but with humility is wisdom."*

Also, Proverbs 29:23 tells us,

> *" A man's pride shall bring him low;*
> *but honour shall uphold the*
> *humble in spirit."*

The moment you kill pride in your life, you have broken the chains of ignorance. This is because the moment you overcome pride you have broken and destroyed ignorance. Only pride can hinder you from destroying ignorance.

And I pray and decree over your life that as you kill pride and stay humble, the chains of ignorance shall be broken in your life, in Jesus' Name. Amen.

iii.   Understand Your Nature in Christ
Understanding your nature in Christ makes you outstanding in life, and also plays a vital role towards breaking the yoke of ignorance in your life.

Understanding your nature in Christ enables you to operate in the supernatural realms far beyond human understanding.

If you understand your nature in Christ, you will realise that the moment you are born again you are not expected to be poor again and that the yoke of ignorance will be broken.

Hear this! When you understand your nature in Christ, the devil loses contact with you and the chains of ignorance will be broken in your life.

iv.   **Read Books**
Reading of books helps in increasing the capacity of your knowledge, and helps you to scale greater heights.

The more you read, the more your mind expands towards making you great in life and will help in breaking the chains of ignorance and other related problems in your life.

Hear this! The best book, one can read, is the Holy Bible, because the Bible is the greatest book of knowledge. You can also read inspirational and motivational books in line with your career and

Chapter 5
BENEFITS OF LIVING A KNOWLEDGEABLE LIFE

*L*iving a knowledgeable life is the ability to influence positive change and the ability to exercise authority over something or person, because you are free and not in captivity or under the mighty chains of ignorance.

Hear this! "To know better is to live better" achieve more accomplishment. They are so many mighty benefits of living a knowledgeable life, but few will be discussed below.

i.   **Being Updated and Current:** This is the first and most foremost benefit of living a knowledgeable life. It guarantees you an updated and relevant information on the things happening around you. Remember, if   you are not informed you will be deformed in life.

The moment you are updated in life, you have the opportunity to be librated in life from poverty to prosperity.

Hear this good news! *"The moment you are updated, you can never be outdated."*

Being updated simply means being current and having the right and needed information, and such information can only be gotten when you go for knowledge. You cannot sit at home without reading books and relevant magazines and expect yourself to be knowledgeable. Rather, you will be ignorant and covered with the canopy of intellectual darkness which is ignorance.

The moment you are current and updated, you will find life meaningful and interesting to you. But when you are ignorant, life will be a frustration and confusion and that will eventually lead to poverty and abject stagnation.

Being current and updated is simply being alive, because the moment you are outdated it simply means you have no life in you; that is to say, you are in the past. That is why to be knowledgeable is very important in all areas of human life and plays a prominent role in our day-to-day activities as children of God, because God is the Father of knowledge.

A wise man once said! ***"If knowledge is difficult ignorance."***

ii.   **Breaking the Chains of Ignorance**

Knowledge is the only vital and powerful key that can unlock the chains of ignorance in one's life. Knowledge is the unlocking of success and prosperity. Knowledge simply means one's ability to know a thing or the possible and best way of using such thing. For example,

You have a Lexus 300 Jeep, which was presented to you by a friend on your wedding day as a gift, and you haven't driven a car in your life before.

You didn't ask your friend anything about how to drive car, and you haven't been to a driving school or learnt to drive a car anywhere.

You rush into the Lexus 300 socket the key and start the car, imagine the car starts to move what will happen?

Hear the truth, you will have a fatal accident because you have been covered by darkness and you are held captive by the chain of ignorance which has made you not to ask the needed question to enable you drive the car. But the moment you are knowledgeable about the driving of a car, may be by going to a driving school or by asking a friend questions on how to drive the car, you could drive it safely without any accident, because you are not under the chains of ignorance.

Without the knowledge of the right word in any area of your life, you will be a failure.

Only the right knowledge can librated you from poverty and make you become successful.

Knowledge is the needed requirement to break the chains of ignorance in one's life, career or business.

iii.   **Being Creative/Innovative**
Being knowledgeable plays a prominent role in one, using one's mind to create new things to achieve a set goal.
Being creative is the divine enablement of the Holy Ghost for us to succeed beyond measure.

Knowledge helps you to use your God-given creativity to transform your life.

Hear this! Creativity goes beyond education.
Being innovative is the function of having the right knowledge. To be innovative simply means to

generate new ideas, methods, procedures in your business and career to enable you be unique; that is, to be the only one of your kind.

Being innovative lies on the kind of knowledge and information one has. Only the right knowledge can enable one to be creative and innovative.

iv.   Being Successful

To be successful simply means making progress were others are struggling to succeed. Being successful is succeeding in a period of economic recession.

To be successful in life simply means you have destroyed the chains of ignorance beyond recognition. Only that right knowledge can enable one to be successful in life and do exploit. Without knowledge in your life, career and business, you can't be successful; rather, you will be wallowing in poverty.

v.   Being Rich

Being knowledgeable simply means having the keys of opportunity in your   hands, and when in one has opportunity, success locates the person, and when success locates you, you are already rich.

Hear This! Right knowledge makes one rich, but wrong knowledge leads to confusion and stagnation which are the brothers of poverty. It is important to note that all knowledge is knowledgeable but right knowledge is preferable.

Knowledge makes one rich both spiritually and physically, and the moment you acquire knowledge you have been liberated from poverty and your dignity will be restored.

vi.   Killing Stagnation

Knowledge is the only bullet that can kill stagnation in one's life. The moment you are knowledgeable in life, stagnation loses contact in your life. Only perfect knowledge can break the yoke of stagnation in ones life.

Stagnation is the force that draws one's destiny to standstill, but knowledge of the right word in the area where one is stagnated can guarantee that the yoke of stagnation will be broken in one's life.

You need to search for knowledge to enable you move forward in life. But when you choose to go for ignorance, stagnation will embrace you and will eventually lead you to poverty and make you captive under its supernatural chains.

Hear this good news! For you to break the powerful chains of ignorance you need the right knowledge. It is critical to note that you can get all the knowledge without knowing how to apply it in the different areas of your life.
Hear this! Only God can direct you on how to apply the right knowledge, and He can direct you, only if you accept Him as your Lord and Saviour. To get connected with God, say this prayer sincerely.

Oh Merciful God, I accept You once again as my God above all on earth and above all forgive me of my sins, wash me with your precious blood, and accept me as your son. Once more, I vow to honour You as my Creator and God above all.

Thank You Lord for saving me, in Jesus' Name. Amen.